# Mr. Insane and the Bandits

## PART 2 OF DADDY'S MAGICAL ADVENTURES SERIES

Mike Patton

NEWMAN SPRINGS PUBLISHING
320 Broad Street
Red Bank, NJ 07701

First originally published by Newman Springs Publishing 2021

ISBN 978-1-63692-376-5 (Paperback)
ISBN 978-1-63692-377-2 (Digital)

Printed in the United States of America

To McKenzie

Daddy and Michaela's bond was definitely getting stronger now that Daddy had the magic dust. No more tossing and turning and turning and tossing all night long for Michaela. Mommy and Daddy living in different cities was not as bad as Michaela had experienced early on. Bedtime was still the best time, knowing that Daddy would be there every night to read her a bedtime story.

Meanwhile on the island of Fogru, things were not so great. Mr. Insane and his group of bandits had arrived on a mission to get the magic dust that Daddy had already taken. His need for it was nothing compared to what Daddy was using the magic dust for. He wanted to use it for pure evil and nothing more. This would help him on his quest to rule the world.

Mr. Insane had come to the island very prepared for his quest to get the magic dust. He had studied the island of Fogru for a very long time. Upon reaching the shore, he was stopped at the gate by Fiddles and Riddles. The moment they showed up, Mr. Insane said, "I have a riddle that not even the two of you can solve."

Fiddles and Riddles were very smart, so they replied, "There is not a riddle that we can't solve."

Mr. Insane turned to the bandits and said, "I don't know which one I should ask…I want to ask the smartest one." It was really a trick. While Fiddles and Riddles argued over who was smarter, Mr. Insane and his bandits were able to easily enter the island of Fogru.

Mr. Insane and his bandits continued with their quest through the island. Just like Daddy, while on his journey to Fogru, Mr. Insane was stopped by Stan and Dan, the two-headed wolves. Before Stan and Dan could get a decent growl out, the bandits shot a net around the two and captured them. Mr. Insane was very taken up with the two and decided to take them home with him. Mr. Insane said, "Load 'em, boys. They'll make very cool pets." So the bandits loaded Stan and Dan on a truck, and then the journey continued.

After walking the path that they studied for years, they made it to Netty—the lost pirate. And just as he told Daddy, Netty bellowed, "No one can gain passage unless they have gold." Mr. Insane gave Netty enough fool's gold to get him and his bandits across the lake twenty times over. Netty took it with pride and gave them passage across the lake.

9

The bandits continued until they reached the coldest part of the island of Fogru. This is where Dila, the frost queen, lived. As they approached, she stopped them just as she did Daddy and said, "Who are you? No one enters my lair...my frost will be the end of you!" Mr. Insane laughed at Dila. His bandits began pulling out flamethrowers. They melted the frost as fast as she was able to make it. Her powers were no match for the bandits. Part of the group kept her occupied while the rest continued forward through the island.

Finally, they reached the darkest part of the island where Lord Ogmar was waiting for them. But before Ogmar could come forward to meet Mr. Insane and the bandits, they turned on lights that lit up the entire area. The light was Lord Ogmar's only weakness. Only Mr. Insane knew about this. This allowed the bandits to capture the dark lord and demanded, "Tell us. Where is the magic dust?"

To their surprise, Ogmar, weakened by the light, whispered, "I no longer have the magic dust. I gave it away some time ago."

13

Mr. Insane didn't believe Ogmar, so he gave the order to the bandits, "Make him talk!" After using evil tactics, Ogmar, the dark lord, showed them an image of the person he gave the magic dust to. It was Daddy.

Mr. Insane took the image and left the island. He took Stan and Dan with him as well. Once Mr. Insane and the bandits got back home, they begin doing research to locate Daddy and claim their prize—the magic dust. Mr. Insane expressed the importance of finding the magic dust to the bandits, "I must have it. With it, I'll be able to take over the world!" He then threatened the bandits, "Find that magic dust by any means necessary." So they continued their research to find Daddy as quickly as possible.

17

Meanwhile, it was getting closer to bedtime, and Michaela was patiently waiting for Daddy to show up. Moments later, like every other night, Daddy magically appeared through the magic dust as he had done every night. Michaela was just as happy as the first day Daddy used the magic dust. "Daddy, Daddy—I knew you'd come. What story are you going to tell me tonight?" Michaela squealed. This was the best time for Michaela, hearing Daddy read her bedtime stories. Daddy read the best stories. He made lots of funny faces and used different voices to make the story come to life.

Back at Mr. Insane's compound, the bandits finally got the break they needed. They were able to get the location of Daddy. So they all packed up and took Mr. Insane's private jet halfway across the world to Danville, Illinois, where Daddy lived. The bandits were instructed to get the magic dust from Daddy—dead or alive. All the bandits joked about the different tortures they would use on Daddy to get the magic dust. As they laughed, you could hear the evil in their voices. This made Mr. Insane smile during the trip as he fed Stan and Dan—his new pets.

In Danville, Daddy was at work and was telling his buddy how he was gonna surprise Michaela and go up for the weekend. Daddy knew that this would make her super happy; his friend agreed. Lionel, Daddy's friend, jokingly asked, "Are you going to use your 'magic dust' to get there?" Lionel thought it was all a big joke but had no idea that Daddy actually had magic dust—and it really did work.

Daddy laughed and told Lionel, "And you have a good weekend too."

Daddy got home and grabbed an overnight bag and sprinkled the magic dust. Moments later, he was in Michaela's town getting a room.

Around the same time back home, Mr. Insane and the bandits had finally made it to Danville. They were en route to daddy's house. To their surprise, nobody was home. This frustrated Mr. Insane in a big way. He screamed at the bandits, "We've come too far. Find him and find him now!"

After pretending that they were friends of Daddy's to some of the neighbors, Mr. Insane and the bandits learned where Daddy worked. Mr. Insane's fake smile turned into a chilling smirk. "I *will* get that magic dust." They quickly made off to Daddy's job. Upon arrival, they found that Daddy was not there either. This really upset Mr. Insane. He had no time to be friendly. He snapped his fingers, and the bandits began roughing up Daddy's coworkers.

One of the bandits grabbed Daddy's friend, Lionel.

"He said he was on his way to see his daughter," Lionel whined.

"Where?" demanded Mr. Insane.

"Milwaukee. Her name is Michaela, and she lives in Milwaukee."

Mr. Insane didn't trust Lionel, so they took him with them. They thought it would be good to have a guide to take them directly to Daddy's location.

Once back onboard Mr. Insane's plane, the bandits placed Lionel in a cage next to Stan and Dan. Mr. Insane knew that the wolves would scare Lionel, and they did just that. Lionel was shivering with fear the whole time. So he told them what they wanted to know, "I remember now. Daddy said he was going on a trip to find some magic dust. Yeah, I thought the dude was just delusional…you know…from the breakup and not seeing his baby girl all the time." Stan and Dan kept growling, and Lionel kept talking. "This magic dust you are looking for, it can't be real. It can't be real," Lionel cried.

Mr. Insane told him that it is very real. "And I plan on getting it and taking over the world with it."

*****

Daddy made it to Michaela's school as she was getting out of class. She was so happy to see him. Not only was she seeing him every night at bedtime, but she had him for the whole weekend as well. On that day, Michaela was the happiest kid in the world. Her daddy meant the world to her, and she glowed. As they walked away, Daddy told her, "We are gonna have the best weekend ever. A weekend filled with adventure. And this time, I won't have to use magic dust to do so."

Mr. Insane and his bandits finally made it to Milwaukee. They had a tour guide. Lionel had gotten Michaela's address off letters she would send to Daddy before leaving the office. Lionel was willing to do anything for the bandits as he feared for his life. The mere thought of capturing Daddy made Mr. Insane smile. He decided he wanted only one thing, so he let Lionel, Stan, and Dan out of the cages. He then began to walk slowly toward Michaela's house. The excitement of getting the magic dust had the bandits chanting along the way, "We'll meet him. We'll beat him. We'll get the dust."

Then they started chanting Mr. Insane's favorite song, "The world will soon change, Mr. Insane. And they will all feel the pain of Mr. Insane. The world's strongest gang is that of Mr. Insane. They will all know the name of Mr. Insane. Mr. Insane, Mr. Insane, Mr. Insane." It was as if the singing motivated them even more to fulfill the mission of getting the magic dust from Daddy.

At last, they reached Michaela's house. Inside the house, Daddy and Michaela were grabbing her bag for the weekend. She had also packed up an extra sack filled with things she felt they would need for the weekend of adventures. Mommy had just left for the weekend moments ago. The two were so happy to be spending time together outside of bedtime stories. But that would soon change. As they opened the door, they were met by Mr. Insane and the bandits.

Daddy and Michaela were startled when they opened the door and saw Mr. Insane and the bandits. Daddy knew this visit by these gruesome-looking people was not intended to be a good one at all. He grabbed Michaela's hand and asked, "How can I help you on this beautiful day?"

Mr. Insane stepped forward and told Daddy, "I do believe you have something that belongs to me. Something I've been searching for, for a very long time. Hand over the magic dust, and I will let you walk away with your life."

Michaela, being an inquisitive child, asked, "Why do you want my daddy's magic dust, and what are you planning to do with it?"

Mr. Insane appeased the inquisitive child and admitted, "I plan to take over the world with it one day at a time, little girl."

Michaela then squeezed daddy's hand tighter. The two looked at each other and knew they had to do something.

Simultaneously, they stepped back and slammed the door on Mr. Insane and the bandits. They then ran upstairs to Michaela's room. In a panicky voice, Michaela asked, "Daddy, what are we gonna do? We can't let them take the magic dust. We just can't, Daddy."

Daddy had the same thought as well. Daddy then grabbed Michaela's hand and told her that he didn't know if this would work, but they had to try. Daddy pulled out the magic dust, and right as he sprinkled it at their feet, one of the bandits ran in and grabbed Michaela before Daddy could vanish with her.

Mr. Insane didn't have the magic dust, but he had something far more valuable to Daddy—his little princess. He knew that Michaela would bring Daddy to him, and this time, he didn't have to look for him. This put that evil grin back on his face again. He told the bandits, "We are done here. Take the girl and let's head home."

Mr. Insane knew the magic dust would find them now, and Daddy would hand it over if he ever wanted to see his daughter again. Mr. Insane praised his bandits for doing such a great job. The bandits went into chanting Mr. Insane's favorite song again as they left for home.

"The world will soon change, Mr. Insane. And they all will feel the pain of Mr. Insane. The world's strongest gang is that of Mr. Insane. They will all know the name of Mr. Insane. Mr. Insane, Mr. Insane, Mr. Insane."

This went on for hours as they headed back to Mr. Insane's castle that was mainly surrounded by water. Once there, they had Lionel call Daddy and tell him that he had twenty-four hours to bring the magic dust or else.

Back home, Daddy kept thinking about how and what he was gonna do to get Michaela back safely. He knew he wouldn't stand a chance against Mr. Insane and his bandits, even with the magic dust. All he could think of was to go back to Fogru to get help. So he sprinkled magic dust and did just that. Upon getting there, he could see that things were wrong. The trolls were still arguing over a riddle. Stan and Dan were gone. Netty was consumed with fool's gold. Dila looked worn out, and Ogmar was injured. Daddy felt bad; he knew this was all his fault.

After helping them all, Ogmar explained why they had to protect the magic dust and how Mr. Insane was actually his brother. "I know him well. He will do no good with it." He told Daddy how Mr. Insane has always been a doer of evil things since they were children. The whole intent of the island was to keep the magic dust from him. He had tried time and time again but had no luck getting through the island. "But this last time, my brother came very prepared."

Daddy then told Ogmar that his brother, Mr. Insane, had his daughter and wanted the magic dust in exchange for her within the next twenty-four hours.

Ogmar told Daddy that he would help him get his little girl back. "I saw firsthand how much she means to you." Ogmar told Daddy that they would need all the help they could get, so he sounded a horn and called everyone on the island to his presence. Fiddles and Riddles came, Netty and Dila came, although there was no Stan and Dan.

Daddy told Ogmar, "They have been captured by Mr. Insane and are being used as his pets."

Lord Ogmar told them the plan to get Michaela, Stan, and Dan back. He told them that the magic dust would not work for all of them and that they would have to travel by boat. This made Netty very happy; his boat was magically fast. They all got on Netty's boat and made it to Mr. Insane's compound in no time. Once there, they all knew exactly what they had to do to get everyone back. Netty would remain on the boat and wait for their return.

Mr. Insane's compound was filled with bandits and heavily lit with bright lights. This would keep Ogmar from entering. Therefore, Dila went around and froze all the lights until they would crack like icicle. This brought complete darkness, and Ogmar was able to come in and take out the bandits with ease. They were no match for the dark lord in the darkness. Mr. Insane could hear the screams as Ogmar got closer to the entrance of the castle.

The doors at the entrance were built to withstand just about anything—anything but the force of two giant trolls Fiddles and Riddles. The two beat the doors until they came falling down. They then entered the castle in search of Mr. Insane. Daddy started yelling Michaela's name, hoping she would answer.

Moments later, she did just that. They all then rushed to her location—in the dungeon, where she was tied up, hanging over a pit of snakes.

Mr. Insane told them that one more move and he would let her fall into the deadly pit. Daddy's heart was racing; he feared for his baby girl's life. He told Mr. Insane that he would do whatever it took to get Michaela back safely. He then told Daddy, "You know what I want, so hand it over."

Michaela yelled, "Daddy, don't do it. He will do bad things with it."

Lord Ogmar, Dila, Fiddles, and Riddles were all staring at Daddy as he pulled out the magic dust. The room was filled with complete silence. Daddy then threw Mr. Insane the magic-dust sack.

Mr. Insane told them that they were all fools and how the world would beg for his mercy. Moments later, he released the rope, letting Michaela fall toward the snake pit. Dila quickly froze the pit, and Daddy caught Michaela while sliding across the ice. The two slid right into Mr. Insane as he was sprinkling the magic dust; then the three of them vanished. Moments later, they reappeared in the cage with Stan and Dan.

The magic dust had dropped and landed right in front of Stan and Dan. The two were growling viciously inside the cage. Mr. Insane thought he could just grab the magic dust, but they tried biting him. Daddy tried to get it, but they tried biting him as well. Then Michaela tried, and the two wolves leaned forward; Daddy's heart nearly stopped. He thought they were gonna bite Michaela, but instead, they licked her hand in a playful manner. They loved the mere sight of children. Michaela then gave the magic dust to Daddy, and the two of them magically left the cage. Mr. Insane was left trapped in the cage with Stan and Dan.

Moments later, Michaela and Daddy appeared in the boat with Ogmar, Dila, Fiddles and Riddles, and Netty. Daddy thanked them all for their help in rescuing his baby girl. Michaela was so fascinated by them all and asked if they were from the magical island of Fogru. After finding this out, she asked Daddy if they could visit them some time. They all seemed to like that idea. Daddy thanked them all again and said he had to get Michaela home before Mommy, so he sprinkled some magic dust, and he and Michaela vanished to her bedroom.

They made it back in perfect timing, just as Mommy was just getting home. Michaela hurried and got in her pajamas, and Daddy grabbed a book. Moments later, Mommy entered and asked the two of them how was their weekend. Michaela replied that it was a very adventurous and magical weekend. Mommy asked Michaela what made it so magical, and she replied, "Daddy's magic dust."

Mommy smiled and told her that she would have to go on a magical adventure with them some time. Daddy and Michaela looked at each other and smiled.

Meanwhile, Mr. Insane and his bandits were taken to the island of Fogru and were locked away so that they couldn't cause any more problems. Even when they were locked up, the bandits still sang Mr. Insane's favorite song from time to time. "The world will soon change, Mr. Insane. And they all will feel the pain of Mr. Insane. The world's strongest gang is that of Mr. Insane. They will all know the name of Mr. Insane, Mr. Insane, Mr. Insane."

The End

CPSIA information can be obtained
at www.ICGtesting.com
Printed in the USA
LVHW071624080222
710592LV00007B/200

9 781636 923765